The Little

WOK

Cookbook

THE LITTLE
WOK
COOKBOOK

HERMES
HOUSE

This edition published by Hermes House
27 West 20th Street, New York, NY 10011

HERMES HOUSE books are available for bulk purchase for sales promotion
and for premium use. For details, write or call the sales director,
Hermes House, 27 West 20th Street, New York, NY 10011;
(800) 354-9657

Hermes House is an imprint of
Anness Publishing Inc.

ISBN 1-84038-400-X

Publisher: Joanna Lorenz
Senior Cookery Editor: Linda Fraser
Assitant Editor: Emma Brown
Copy Editor: Jenni Fleetwood
Designer: Patrick McLeavey
Illustrator: Anna Koska
Photographers: Michelle Garrett, James Duncan, Edward Allwright &
Amanda Heywood
Recipes: Liz Trigg, Catherine Atkinson, Deh-Ta Hsiung, Steven Wheeler &
Shirley Gill

Printed and bound in Singapore

Contents

Introduction

Where would we be without the wok? It is probably the single most useful pan in the kitchen. The deep bowl and angled sides make it ideal for stir-frying, steaming and braising. It can be used to make soups, rice and noodle dishes, is handy for deep-frying dumplings and can even be used to toss a hot salad.

Wok cookery is generally healthy. Stir-fries usually consist largely of vegetables, with a small amount of high quality protein, and the rapid cooking means that more nutrients are retained and fat-absorption is limited. Steamed foods lose a small amount of nutrients to the water, but the water can be used as the basis for a soup.

Small wonder that the wok grows more popular by the day – and not just for Chinese and Thai cooking. A number of of the recipes in this collection, including Glazed Lamb and Stir-fried Duck with Blueberries, have no association with Asian cuisine, but nevertheless owe their superb flavor to speedy wok cooking.

For anyone whose kitchen facilities are limited, a wok is a real boon. You cook in it, serve from it, and it is easy to clean. Season a new wok properly and it will only need rinsing in hot water before being dried, oiled and put away.

Woks come in a range of materials, at prices for all budgets, alone or in boxed sets with accessories. For even heating and durability, the basic carbon steel wok – the kind you see in Chinese stores the world over — remains the best value. Pau woks (one handle) are designed for stir-frying, while twin-handled Cantonese woks are preferred for steaming and deep-frying.

Very few accessories are required. A couple of sharp knives — a small vegetable knife and a flat-bladed cook's knife — will be adequate for preparing ingredients, although those who have become familiar with the cleaver find this kitchen tool indispensable. Not only does it chop, dice, slice and crush (ginger and garlic) but the blade can be used to transport the food to the wok.

It is convenient to have several cutting boards (some Chinese cooks use sections of tree trunk). For turning food when stir-frying, traditionalists

use a long-handled forged iron ladle with a matching turner (shaped to the curve of the wok), but a couple of wooden spoons, or a spoon and spatula, can be used instead. A skimmer is useful, but you can substitute a slotted spoon.

Improvisation is the name of the game when it comes to wok cooking. If you like the look of a recipe, but haven't got the requisite ingredients, substitute. Just remember that colors, flavors and textures should be in balance.

Wok cooking is so rapid that every-thing must be ready before you begin. Mix marinades, measure out sauces and flavorings, and arrange all the ingredients in order of use. Having set the scene, relax and enjoy yourself. Wok cooking is a lot of fun!

Ingredients

CHINESE EGG NOODLES
Available fresh and dried, these come in various widths and are sold in bundles. They take very little time to cook and may need merely a quick dip in boiling water before serving. Follow the instructions on the package.

SESAME OIL
An aromatic oil used for adding flavor to foods near the end of cooking. Sesame oil can be used for stir-frying but burns easily, so is best mixed with sunflower oil.

GRAPESEED OIL
With its delicate flavor, this light oil will not mask the taste of stir-fried ingredients.

RICE WINE
Made from fermented steamed white rice, this popular drink is often used to flavor stir-fries. If unavailable, substitute dry sherry.

CHILI SAUCE
This bottled sauce is a very hot blend of chilies, vinegar and salt. Use sparingly. For a milder flavor, use sweet chili sauce.

BEAN SAUCE
Both yellow and black bean sauces are made from ground soy beans fermented with flour and salt. Black bean sauce has a stronger flavor and is often used with seafood.

SOY SAUCE
Available in various strengths, light soy sauce has more flavor than the sweeter dark soy sauce. Japanese shoyu has a different, very distinctive taste.

OYSTER SAUCE
This savory sauce is made from oysters and juice, with water, sugar, salt and starch. It enhances the flavor of meat and vegetable dishes without making them taste fishy.

8

DRIED BLACK CHINESE MUSHROOMS AND FUNGI

Although these look rather uninteresting when dry, they plump up when soaked in water for 25–30 minutes and make a delicious addition to stir-fries. Discard the stem. Wood Ears and Cloud Ears are popular dried black fungi. When they are soaked in water they look gelatinous but taste crunchy.

BAMBOO SHOOTS

Young bamboo shoots have a delicate flavor. They are available canned, in large chunks or thin slices. Drain well before use.

LEMONGRASS

Fresh lemongrass has a wonderful citrus flavor. In stir-fries it is often used whole, in which case the stem is bruised and the grass then removed before serving. Alternately, the lower part of the stem can be chopped or sliced before being stir-fried.

GINGER

Fresh ginger adds fragrance and flavor. Store it in the fridge (wrapped in plastic wrap or peeled, sliced and in sherry) or freeze it. Frozen ginger grates easily and does not need peeling.

9

CILANTRO

This leafy green herb is a very common accompaniment to Asian meat and fish dishes. It is sometimes called Chinese parsley, coriander or Greek parsley. It is intensely aromatic.

BEAN CURD

Also known as tofu, this is made from processed soy beans and is highly nutritious. Various forms are available, from a light creamy tofu (ideal for dips or desserts) to a firm type, which may be plain, flavored or smoked. Firm tofu is ideal for stir-frying as it retains its shape when cooked.

Techniques

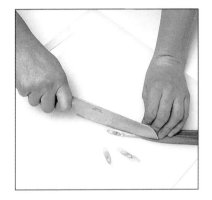

SEASONING THE WOK

Seasoning, in this instance, has nothing to do with salt and pepper. It's a technique for preparing a new pan for use, so that ingredients do not stick to its surface in the future. Wash and dry the wok thoroughly. Pour a little oil into the wok and spread it around to coat the inside, using a wad of paper towels. Keep rubbing the surface until the paper comes away clean. Place the pan over high heat until very hot, then cool.

CLEANING THE WOK

Rinse the wok with hot water, scrub lightly with a bamboo brush or non-abrasive scrub pad and dry thoroughly with paper towels or over medium heat. To prevent rusting, coat the wok lightly with oil before storing.

PREPARING INGREDIENTS

So that food cooks quickly and evenly, cut it into small pieces of uniform size. Slice meats, leafy vegetables and mushrooms across the grain, celery and scallions diagonally. Alternately, cut vegetables into julienne strips (thin matchsticks).

SIMPLE STIR-FRYING

Start by heating a clean, dry wok. When it is hot, drizzle a "necklace" of oil all around the inner rim, give it a few seconds to coat the wok and heat through, then add the ingredients in order, with those that require the most cooking first. Using a ladle and turner or two wooden spoons, toss all the ingredients over the heat as when mixing a salad. Add seasonings at the end of cooking.

BAO

This is a method of rapid stir-frying which takes its name from a Chinese word meaning "to explode." The food is cooked very quickly over intense heat, so any ingredients that are likely to need longer cooking are parboiled or steamed in advance. Marinades and sauces are sometimes used.

STIR-BRAISING

In this method of cooking, the main ingredient, such as meat or poultry, is cooked first, then removed from the wok while vegetables and seasonings are stir-fried. All the ingredients are then brought together with sauces and stock, thickened with cornstarch and rapidly braised before serving.

DEEP-FRYING

The best style of wok for deep-frying is the Cantonese twin-handled type, with a deep bowl. It is essential that the wok is completely stable; unless the wok is flat-bottomed you may need to use a stand. Do not preheat the wok before adding the oil, and fill to no more than half full. Add only a few items at a time, and never leave the wok unattended. Keep a lid nearby. Use a skimmer or a slotted spoon to remove cooked food.

STEAMING

Many wok sets come complete with steamer racks. You can also buy bamboo stacking steamers, which are very useful, as you can steam several foods simultaneously. Cover the top steamer with a bamboo lid or foil. Alternately, improvise by using a metal trivet topped with a plate. Cover with the domed lid of the wok and steam the food until tender, adding water as required.

11

COOK'S TIP

To toss a hot salad: Stir-fry bacon with onion, celery and garlic in a little oil, then push these ingredients to the sides of the wok. Add just enough red wine vinegar and soy sauce to the oil and bacon fat to make a flavorful dressing, then add the torn leaves of a head of Iceberg lettuce. Toss swiftly with the other ingredients and serve immediately.

Appetizers

Corn & Chicken Soup

INGREDIENTS

1 chicken breast, about 4 ounces, cubed
2 teaspoons light soy sauce
1 tablespoon Chinese rice wine
1 teaspoon cornstarch
4 tablespoons cold water
1 teaspoon sesame oil
2 tablespoons peanut oil
1 teaspoon grated fresh ginger
4 cups chicken stock
1 can (15 ounces) creamed corn
1 can (8 ounces) corn kernels
2 eggs, beaten
2-3 scallions, green parts only, cut in thin rounds
salt and freshly ground black pepper

SERVES 4–6

1 Grind all the chicken roughly in a food processor. Transfer to a bowl and stir in the soy sauce, rice wine, cornstarch, water, sesame oil and seasoning. Cover and let stand for 15 minutes. Heat a wok, add the peanut oil and stir-fry the ginger briefly.

2 Add the stock and all the corn to the wok. When almost boiling, stir about 6 tablespoons of the hot liquid into the chicken mixture until it forms a smooth paste. Add this to the wok. Slowly bring to a boil, stirring constantly, then simmer for 2–3 minutes.

3 Pour in the beaten eggs in a slow, steady stream, using a fork or chopsticks to stir the top of the soup in a figure-eight pattern. The egg should cook in lacy strands. Serve immediately, with the scallions sprinkled on top.

13

Spiced Scallops in their Shells

INGREDIENTS

8 scallops, shelled, plus the cupped side of
4 shells
2 slices fresh ginger, diced
½ garlic clove, diced
2 scallions, green parts only, thinly sliced
salt and freshly ground black pepper
SAUCE
1 garlic clove, crushed
1 tablespoon grated fresh ginger
2 scallions, white parts only, chopped
1-2 fresh green chilies, seeded
and finely chopped
1 tablespoon light soy sauce
1 tablespoon dark soy sauce
2 teaspoons sesame oil

SERVES 4

14

1 Remove the dark beard-like fringe and tough muscle from the scallops.

2 Place two scallops in each shell. Season with a little salt and pepper, then scatter the ginger, garlic and scallions on top. Place the shells in a bamboo  steamer and steam for about 6 minutes until the scallops look opaque (you may have to do this in batches if your steamer is a small one).

3 Make the sauce. Combine the diced garlic, fresh ginger, scallions, chilies, light soy sauce, dark soy sauce and sesame oil and stir well, until thoroughly blended. Pour the sauce into a small serving bowl.

4 Lift each shell out of the bamboo steamer — be careful not to spill any of the juices. Arrange them on a large plate with the sauce bowl in the center. Serve.

Thai Fish Cakes

INGREDIENTS

*1 pound white-fish fillets, such as cod
or haddock
3 scallions, sliced
2 tablespoons chopped fresh cilantro
2 tablespoons Thai red curry paste
1 fresh green chili, seeded and chopped
2 teaspoons grated lime rind
1 tablespoon lime juice
2 tablespoons peanut oil
salt, to taste
crisp lettuce leaves, shredded scallions,
fresh red chili slices, cilantro sprigs
and lime wedges, to serve*

SERVES 4

1 Cut the fish into chunks, then place in a blender or food processor. Add the sliced scallions, cilantro, red curry paste, green chili, lime rind and lime juice to the fish. Season with salt. Process until finely ground.

2 Divide the mixture into 16 pieces and shape each one into a small cake, 1½ inches across (flouring your hands lightly may help). Arrange all the fish cakes

on a plate, cover with plastic wrap and chill for 2 hours, until firm. Heat the wok over fairly high heat until hot. Add the oil and swirl it around.

3 Fry the fish cakes, in batches, for 6–8 minutes, turning them over only once, until evenly browned. Drain each batch on paper towels and keep hot while

cooking the rest of the cakes. Serve on a bed of crisp lettuce leaves with shredded scallions, red chili slices, cilantro sprigs and lime wedges.

16

Eggplant with Sesame Chicken

INGREDIENTS

1 skinless, boneless chicken breast (6 ounces)
1 scallion, green part only, finely chopped
1 tablespoon dark soy sauce
1 tablespoon Mirin or sweet sherry
½ teaspoon sesame oil
¼ teaspoon salt
4 small eggplants, about 4 inches long
1 tablespoon sesame seeds
flour, for dusting
vegetable oil, for deep-frying
cucumber and carrot shapes, to garnish
DIPPING SAUCE
4 tablespoons dark soy sauce
4 tablespoons Dashi or vegetable stock
3 tablespoons Mirin or sweet sherry

SERVES 4

17

1 Make the stuffing. Grind the chicken finely in a food processor. Add the scallion, soy sauce, Mirin, sesame oil and salt. Make four slits in each eggplant, keeping them joined at the stem. Spoon the stuffing into the slits.

2 Dip each stuffed eggplant in the sesame seeds, then dust in flour. Set the eggplants aside. Make the dipping sauce by mixing the soy sauce, Dashi and Mirin in a shallow bowl.

3 Heat the vegetable oil in a wok to 385°F. Fry the eggplants, two at a time, for about 3–4 minutes. Lift out with a slotted spoon onto paper towels to drain. Serve the eggplants at once, garnished with a few of the cucumber and carrot shapes.

Crispy Vegetable Spring Rolls

INGREDIENTS

4 ounces young leeks or scallions
4 ounces carrots
1 cup bamboo shoots
1 cup mushrooms
2 cups fresh beansprouts
3-4 tablespoons vegetable oil
1 teaspoon salt
1 teaspoon light brown sugar
1 tablespoon light soy sauce
1 tablespoon Chinese rice wine or dry sherry
20 frozen spring-roll skins, thawed
4 tablespoons cornstarch mixed to a paste with
5 tablespoons water
flour, for dusting
oil, for deep-frying
dipping sauce, such as soy sauce, to serve

MAKES 40 ROLLS

1 Cut all the vegetables into thin sticks, roughly the same size and shape as the bean sprouts.

2 Heat the oil in a wok and stir-fry the vegetables for about 1 minute. Add the salt, sugar, soy sauce and wine or sherry and heat through, stirring for 1½–2 minutes. Remove and drain off the excess liquid, then let cool.

3 To make the spring rolls, cut each spring-roll skin in half diagonally, then place 1 tablespoon of the vegetable mixture one-third of the way up on the spring-roll skin, with the triangle pointing away from you. Lift the long lower edge over the filling and roll once to enclose the filling.

4 Fold in both ends and roll once more, then brush the upper edge with a little cornstarch paste, and roll into a neat package. Dust a large plate with flour and place the spring rolls on it, flap-sides down. Cover loosely and set aside until needed.

5 To cook, heat the oil in a wok until hot, then reduce the heat to low. Deep-fry the spring rolls in batches (about 8–10 at a time) for 2–3 minutes, or until golden and crispy, then lift out and drain on paper towels. Serve the spring rolls hot with a dipping sauce, such as soy sauce.

Fish & Shellfish Dishes

Fragrant Swordfish with Ginger & Lemongrass

INGREDIENTS

1 kaffir lime leaf
3 tablespoons sea salt
5 tablespoons light brown sugar
4 swordfish steaks (about 8 ounces each)
1 lemongrass stalk, sliced
1 inch fresh ginger, cut in matchsticks
1 lime
1 tablespoon grapeseed oil
1 large ripe avocado
salt and ground black pepper
lime slices, to garnish

SERVES 4

1 Bruise the lime leaf by crushing it slightly to release the flavor. Make a marinade by processing the sea salt, brown sugar and lime leaf in a food processor, until thoroughly blended.

2 Place the sword-fish steaks in a bowl. Sprinkle the marinade over them and add the lemongrass and ginger. Cover and let marinate for 3–4 hours.

3 Rinse off the marinade and pat the fish dry with paper towels. Pare the rind from the lime. Remove any excess pith, then cut it into very thin strips.

4 Heat the wok, then add the oil. When hot, add the lime rind, then the steaks, and stir-fry for 3–4 minutes. Add the lime juice. Remove from the heat. Cut the avo-

cado in half, remove the pit, peel the skin, and slice thinly. Season the fish and serve with the avocado, garnished with lime slices.

Sweet-&-Sour Fish

INGREDIENTS

1 pound white-fish fillets, skinned, boned
and cubed
½ teaspoon Chinese five-spice powder
1 teaspoon light soy sauce
1 egg, lightly beaten
2-3 tablespoons cornstarch
peanut oil, for deep-frying
SAUCE
2 teaspoons cornstarch
4 tablespoons water
4 tablespoons pineapple juice
3 tablespoons Chinese rice vinegar
3 tablespoons sugar
2 teaspoons light soy sauce
2 tablespoons ketchup
2 teaspoons Chinese rice wine or dry sherry
3 tablespoons peanut oil
1 garlic clove, crushed
1 tablespoon chopped fresh ginger
6 scallions, sliced diagonally in
2-inch lengths
1 green bell pepper, seeded and cut in
¾-inch squares
4 ounces fresh pineapple, cubed
salt and freshly ground black pepper

SERVES 3–4

1 Put the fish in a bowl. Sprinkle on the five-spice powder and soy sauce, then toss gently. Cover and let marinate for 30 minutes. Dip the fish in the egg, then in the cornstarch, coating it all over. Shake off any excess cornstarch.

2 Half-fill a wok with oil and heat to 375°F. Deep-fry the fish in batches for 2 minutes until golden. Drain and keep hot. Carefully pour out the oil and wipe the wok clean.

3 Make the sauce. Blend the cornstarch, water, pineapple juice, rice vinegar, sugar, soy sauce, ketchup and rice wine or dry sherry in a bowl. Mix well, then set aside.

4 Heat the wok until hot, add 2 tablespoons of the oil and swirl it around. Add the garlic and ginger and stir-fry for a few seconds. Add the scallions and green pepper squares and stir-fry over medium heat for 2 minutes. Add the pineapple.

5 Stir in the cornstarch mixture. Cook until thick. Stir in the remaining oil and add seasoning to taste. Pour the sauce over the fish and serve.

Ragoût of Shellfish with Sweet Scented Basil

INGREDIENTS

12 fresh mussels in their shells, scrubbed
4 tablespoons water
1⅔ cups canned coconut milk
1¼ cups chicken stock
8 ounces prepared squid, cut in strips
12 ounces monkfish, skinned
5 ounces cooked shrimp, peeled and deveined
4 scallops, sliced (optional)
½ cup canned bamboo shoots, drained
½ cup green beans, blanched
1 ripe tomato, peeled, seeded and roughly chopped
4 large-leaf basil sprigs, torn, to garnish
boiled rice and chili sauce, to serve
GREEN CURRY PASTE
2 teaspoons coriander seeds
½ teaspoon caraway or cumin seeds
3-4 medium green chilies, finely chopped
4 teaspoons sugar
2 teaspoons salt
1 piece lemongrass, 3 inches long
2 tablespoons finely chopped fresh ginger
3 garlic cloves
1 onion, finely chopped
1 piece shrimp paste, ¾ inch square
1 cup cilantro leaves, finely chopped
3 tablespoons finely chopped fresh basil leaves
2 tablespoons vegetable oil

SERVES 4–6

1 Put the mussels in a large saucepan, add the water, cover and cook for 6–8 minutes until the mussels open (discard any that remain closed). Take two-thirds of them out of their shells. Set all the mussels aside, with the strained cooking liquid.

2 Make the curry paste. Dry-fry all the seeds in a wok to release their flavor. Grind the chilies to a smooth paste with the sugar and salt. Add the seeds, lemongrass, ginger, garlic and onion, and grind until smooth. Stir in the shrimp paste, herbs and vegetable oil.

3 Strain the coconut milk into a wok, reserving the solids in the strainer. Add the stock and about 4 tablespoons of the green curry paste to the wok (keep the remaining paste in a covered jar in the fridge, for another occasion). Boil rapidly until the liquid is reduced by half.

4 Stir in all the squid, fish and coconut solids, then simmer for 15–20 minutes. Add the shellfish, bamboo shoots, beans, and tomato and simmer for  2–3 minutes. Season, then serve, garnished with basil, accompanied by boiled rice and chili sauce.

24

Quick-fried Shrimp with Hot Spices

INGREDIENTS

1 pound large uncooked shrimp
1 inch fresh ginger, grated
2 garlic cloves, crushed
1 teaspoon hot chili powder
1 teaspoon ground turmeric
2 teaspoons black mustard seeds
seeds from 4 green cardamom pods, crushed
4 tablespoons ghee or butter
½ cup coconut milk
salt and freshly ground black pepper
chopped fresh cilantro, to garnish
naan, to serve

SERVES 2–4

1 Peel the shrimp carefully, leaving the tails attached. Using a small sharp knife, make a slit along the back of each shrimp and then remove the dark
vein. Rinse all the shrimp under cold running water, drain and pat dry with paper towels.

2 Put the ginger, garlic, chili powder, turmeric, mustard seeds and cardamom seeds in a bowl. Add the shrimp and toss to coat with the spice mixture.

3 Heat a wok until hot. Add the ghee or butter and swirl it around until foaming.

4 Add the spiced shrimp. Stir-fry them for about 1–1½ minutes until they are just turning pink. Stir in the coconut milk and simmer for 3–4 minutes
until the shrimp are cooked. Season with salt and pepper, then sprinkle on the cilantro, to garnish. Serve immediately with naan.

Squid with Peppers in a Black Bean Sauce

INGREDIENTS

2 tablespoons salted black beans
2 tablespoons medium-dry sherry
1 tablespoon light soy sauce
1 teaspoon cornstarch
$\frac{1}{2}$ teaspoon sugar
2 tablespoons water
3 tablespoons peanut oil
1 pound prepared squid, scored and cut in
thick strips
1 teaspoon finely chopped fresh ginger
1 garlic clove, finely chopped
1 fresh green chili, seeded and sliced
6-8 scallions, cut diagonally in
short lengths
$\frac{1}{2}$ red and $\frac{1}{2}$ green bell pepper, cored, seeded
and cut in 1-inch diamonds
$\frac{3}{4}$ cup shiitake mushrooms,
thickly sliced

SERVES 4

2 Heat a wok, add the oil, then stir-fry the squid briefly, until opaque. Remove with a slotted spoon.

3 Add the ginger, garlic and chili to the wok. Stir-fry briefly, then add the vegetables and stir-fry for 2 minutes. Toss in the squid and the black bean sauce.

1 Rinse the black beans thoroughly and finely chop them. Place them in a bowl with the sherry, soy sauce, cornstarch, sugar and water; mix well.

Cook, stirring, for about 1 minute or until thickened. Serve the stir-fry immediately.

Poultry Dishes

Stir-fried Duck with Blueberries

INGREDIENTS

2 duck breasts (6 ounces each)
2 tablespoons sunflower oil
1 tablespoon red wine vinegar
1 teaspoon sugar
1 teaspoon red wine
1 teaspoon crème de cassis
1 cup fresh blueberries
1 tablespoon chopped fresh mint
salt and freshly ground black pepper
fresh mint sprigs, to garnish
sliced celery and scallion salad, to serve

SERVES 4

2 Stir in the fresh blueberries. Gently heat through, then sprinkle the mint on top. Serve immediately, garnished with mint sprigs, and the celery and scallion salad.

1 With a cleaver or a sharp knife, cut both duck breasts in neat thin slices. Season the duck generously, then heat the wok and add the oil. When the oil is hot, stir-fry the duck slices for 3 minutes. Add the red wine vinegar, sugar, red wine and crème de cassis. Boil for about 3 minutes, to reduce the liquid to a thick syrup.

29

Turkey with Sage, Prunes & Brandy

INGREDIENTS

½ cup prunes
1 turkey breast (3–3½ pounds)
1 tablespoon fresh sage, chopped
1¼ cups cognac or brandy
5 ounces slab bacon, in one piece
4 tablespoons butter
24 baby onions, peeled and quartered
salt and freshly ground black pepper
fresh sage sprigs, to garnish

SERVES 4

1 Pit the prunes and cut them into slivers. Remove the skin from the turkey and cut the breast into thin pieces.

2 Combine the prunes, sage, turkey and cognac or brandy in a non-metallic dish. Cover and let marinate in the fridge for 6–8 hours, or overnight.

3 Strain the turkey and prunes, reserving the cognac mixture, and pat dry with paper towels.

4 Cut the bacon into lardoons (dice), place them on a plate and set aside. Heat the wok and add half the butter. When melted, add the baby onion quarters and stir-fry for about 4 minutes, until they are crisp and golden brown. Set aside.

5 Heat the wok, and stir-fry the bacon lardoons for 1 minute. Stir until they release some fat. Add the remaining butter and stir-fry the turkey for about 3–4 minutes, until crisp and golden. Add the prunes and stir-fry briefly. Push the turkey mixture to one side in the wok and add the cognac mixture; simmer until thickened. Stir the turkey into the sauce, season well with salt and pepper, and serve the stir-fry immediately, garnished with sprigs of fresh sage.

Glazed Chicken with Cashews

INGREDIENTS

¾ cup cashews
3 tablespoons peanut oil
4 garlic cloves, finely chopped
1 red bell pepper, halved, seeded and
sliced in strips
1 pound skinless, boneless chicken breasts,
cut in strips
2 tablespoons Chinese rice wine or medium-
dry sherry
3 tablespoons hoisin sauce
2 teaspoons sesame oil
5-6 scallions, green parts only, sliced
soy sauce, to serve

SERVES 4

2 Heat the wok again until hot, add the oil and swirl it around. Add the garlic and let it sizzle for a few seconds. Add the red pepper and chicken strips, and

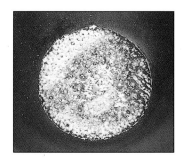

stir-fry over fairly high heat for 2 minutes. Do not let the garlic scorch, or it will taste bitter.

3 Pour the rice wine or sherry and the hoisin sauce over the chicken mixture and stir well. Continue to stir-fry until the chicken is tender and evenly glazed.

1 Heat a wok until hot, then add the cashews and stir-fry over low to medium heat for 1–2 minutes, or until golden brown. Remove and set aside.

4 Stir in the sesame oil, and then sprinkle the cashews and scallions over the stir-fry. Toss quickly to mix, then serve with soy sauce.

Spicy Clay Pot Chicken

INGREDIENTS

1 chicken (3-3½ pounds)
3 tablespoons freshly-grated coconut
2 tablespoons vegetable oil
1 small onion, finely chopped
2 garlic cloves, crushed
1 piece galangal or fresh ginger, 1 inch long,
peeled and thinly sliced
2 small green chilies, seeded and finely chopped
1 tablespoon fish sauce or 1 piece shrimp paste,
½ inch square
1 piece lemongrass, 2 inches long
1⅔ cups canned coconut milk
1¼ cups chicken stock
2 lime leaves (optional)
1 tablespoon sugar
1 tablespoon rice or white wine vinegar
2 ripe tomatoes, to garnish
2 tablespoons chopped cilantro leaves,
to garnish
boiled rice, to serve

SERVES 6

1 To prepare the chicken, remove the legs and wings with a chopping knife. Skin the pieces and separate the drumsticks from the thighs. Using kitchen scissors, cut the breast from the body and cut it into four pieces. Set the chicken aside.

2 Dry-fry all the coconut in a large wok until evenly browned. Add the vegetable oil with the onion, garlic, galangal or ginger, chilies, fish sauce and lemongrass. Fry briefly over medium to high heat to release all the flavors.

3 Preheat the oven to 350°F. Add the chicken pieces to the wok and brown evenly with the spices for 2–3 minutes.

4 Strain the coconut milk and add the thin part to the wok with the chicken stock, lime leaves if using, sugar and vinegar. Stir well and bring to a boil. Transfer to a glazed clay pot or casserole, cover and bake for 50–55 minutes, or until the chicken is tender. Stir in the thick part of the coconut milk and return to the oven for about 5–10 minutes to simmer and thicken.

5 Place the tomatoes in a bowl and cover with boiling water to loosen and remove the skins. Halve the tomatoes, remove the seeds and cut into large dice. Add the tomatoes to the finished dish, scatter with the chopped cilantro and serve immediately, with a large bowl of boiled rice.

Meat Dishes

Glazed Lamb

INGREDIENTS

1 tablespoon grapeseed oil
*1 pound boneless lean lamb, cut in thin
neat strips*
6 ounces sugar snap peas, trimmed
3 scallions, sliced
2 tablespoons honey
juice of ½ lemon
*2 tablespoons chopped fresh cilantro, plus extra
sprigs to garnish*
1 tablespoon sesame seeds
salt and freshly ground black pepper
lemon wedges, to serve

SERVES 4

2 Add the sugar snap peas and scallions to the hot wok and stir-fry for about 30 seconds.

1 Heat the wok, then add the oil. When the oil is hot, stir-fry the lamb strips until browned all over. Remove the lamb from the wok and keep it hot.

3 Return the lamb to the wok and add the honey, lemon juice, cilantro and sesame seeds. Season and stir-fry briefly. Serve with lemon wedges, garnished with herbs.

Stir-fried Lamb with Scallions

INGREDIENTS

*1 leg of lamb (12-14 ounces),
thinly sliced
1 teaspoon light brown sugar
1 tablespoon light soy sauce
1 tablespoon Chinese rice wine or dry sherry
2 teaspoons cornstarch, mixed to a paste with
1 tablespoon water
½ ounce dried black wood ears
about 4 tablespoons vegetable oil
6-8 scallions, thickly sliced
a few small pieces fresh ginger
2 tablespoons yellow bean sauce
a few drops sesame oil*

SERVES 4

1 Marinate the lamb with the sugar, soy sauce, wine or sherry and cornstarch paste for 30–45 minutes. Soak the wood ears in water for 25–30 minutes, then cut into small pieces.

2 Heat the oil in a large wok until hot and stir-fry the meat for about 2–3 minutes, or until lightly browned. Remove with a slotted spoon and drain.

3 Keep about 1 tablespoon of oil in the wok, then add all the scallions, the ginger, wood ears and yellow bean sauce. Blend well, then add the meat and stir-fry for about 1 minute. Sprinkle the sesame oil over the top, toss to mix, and serve immediately.

Stir-fried Pork with Vegetables

INGREDIENTS

8 ounces pork fillet, thinly sliced
1 tablespoon light soy sauce, plus extra to taste
1 teaspoon light brown sugar
1 teaspoon Chinese rice wine or dry sherry
2 teaspoons cornstarch, mixed to a paste with
1 tablespoon water
4 tablespoons vegetable oil
1 cup sugar snap peas,
trimmed
1 cup white mushrooms,
thinly sliced
1 medium or 2 small carrots, thinly sliced
1 scallion, sliced
1 teaspoon salt
chicken stock or water, if necessary
a few drops sesame oil

SERVES 4

1 Marinate the pork with the soy sauce, sugar, wine or sherry and cornstarch paste.

2 Heat the oil in a preheated wok and stir-fry the pork for 2–3 minutes, or until lightly browned. Remove and keep warm.

3 Stir-fry all the vegetables together for 2 minutes, then add the salt and pork, with a little stock or water, if necessary. Stir-fry for 1 more minute, then season with  soy sauce, to taste. Sprinkle the sesame oil over the top and serve immediately.

39

Stir-fried Pork with Mustard

INGREDIENTS

3 tablespoons unsalted butter
1 cooking apple, peeled, cored and thinly sliced
1 tablespoon sugar
1 1/4 pounds pork fillet, thinly sliced
1 small onion, finely chopped
2 tablespoons Calvados or other brandy
1 tablespoon coarse-grain mustard
2/3 cup heavy cream
2 tablespoons chopped fresh parsley
Italian parsley sprigs, to garnish

SERVES 4

1 Heat the wok, then add half the butter. When the butter is hot, add the apple slices, sprinkle on the sugar, and stir-fry for 2–3 minutes. Remove the apple slices and set them aside. Wipe out the wok with paper towels and return it to the stove.

2 Heat the wok, then add the remaining butter and stir-fry the pork and onion for 2–3 minutes, until the pork is golden and the onion tender.

3 Stir in the Calvados or other brandy and boil until it is reduced by half. Stir in the mustard.

4 Add the cream, stir to mix well, and simmer for about 1 minute. Add the chopped parsley. Stir, then serve, with a few sprigs of parsley to garnish.

COOK'S TIP

Use bamboo chopsticks as Chinese cooks do: for moving food around in the wok, for beating eggs or for lifting deep-fried items.

Sukiyaki-style Beef

INGREDIENTS

7 ounces Japanese rice noodles
1 tablespoon shredded suet
1 pound thick round steak, thinly sliced
7 ounces hard tofu, cut in cubes
8 shiitake mushrooms, trimmed
2 leeks, sliced in 1-inch lengths
salt
*3 cups baby spinach
leaves, to serve*
STOCK
1 tablespoon sugar
6 tablespoons rice wine
3 tablespoons dark soy sauce
½ cup water

SERVES 4

1 Bring a saucepan of lightly salted water to a boil. Add the noodles and blanch for 2 minutes. Drain well. Mix all the stock ingredients in a bowl.

2 Heat the wok, then add the suet. Let it melt, then add the beef and stir-fry for 2–3 minutes. It should be cooked but still fairly pink in color.

3 Pour the stock over the beef. Add the rest of the ingredients. Cook for 4 minutes or until the leeks are tender. Serve a selection of all the ingredients to each person, with a few baby spinach leaves. It is not necessary to add a garnish.

Beef with Cantonese Oyster Sauce

INGREDIENTS

10-12 ounces beef steak, thinly sliced
1 teaspoon light brown sugar
1 tablespoon light soy sauce
2 teaspoons Chinese rice wine or dry sherry
2 teaspoons cornstarch, mixed to a paste with
1 tablespoon water
4 tablespoons vegetable oil
1 scallion, sliced
a few small pieces fresh ginger
1 cup sugar snap peas,
trimmed
1 cup baby corn, halved
1 cup drained canned
straw mushrooms
1/2 teaspoon salt
2 tablespoons oyster sauce

SERVES 4

44

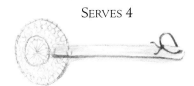

1 In a bowl, marinate the beef with the sugar, soy sauce, rice wine or sherry and cornstarch paste for 25–30 minutes, stirring the mixture occasionally.

2 Heat the oil in a large wok and fry the beef for 2–3 minutes, until lightly browned. Remove the beef with a slotted spoon and drain.

3 Pour off the excess oil, leaving 2 tablespoons in the wok, and add the scallion, ginger, vegetables and salt. Stir-fry for 2–3 minutes, then return the beef

slices to the wok. Add the oyster sauce. Blend well and serve immediately.

Stir-fried Beef & Broccoli

INGREDIENTS

12 ounces round steak
1 tablespoon cornstarch
1 teaspoon sesame oil
12 ounces broccoli, cut in small florets
4 scallions, sliced diagonally
1 carrot, cut in matchstick strips
1 garlic clove, crushed
1 inch fresh ginger, cut in very
fine strips
½ cup beef stock
2 tablespoons soy sauce
2 tablespoons dry sherry
2 teaspoons light brown sugar
scallion curls, to garnish
egg noodles or rice, to serve

SERVES 4

1 Trim the beef and cut into thin slices across the grain. Cut each slice into thin strips. Toss in the cornstarch to coat thoroughly. Heat the sesame oil in a wok. Add the beef strips and stir-fry over high heat for 3 minutes. Remove and set aside.

2 Add the broccoli, scallions, carrot, garlic clove, ginger strips and beef stock to the wok. Cover and simmer for 3 minutes. Remove the lid and cook, stirring, until the stock has evaporated, leaving behind the flavored vegetable mixture.

3 Combine the soy sauce, sherry and brown sugar. Add the mixture to the wok, then add the beef. Cook for 2–3 minutes, stirring continuously. Spoon into a warm serving dish and garnish with scallion curls. Serve with egg noodles or rice.

45

Vegetable Dishes

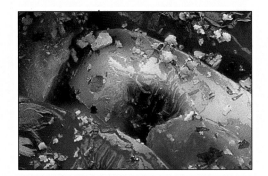

Bok Choy & Mushroom Stir-fry

INGREDIENTS

4 dried black Chinese mushrooms
½ cup boiling water
1 tablespoon vegetable oil
1 garlic clove, crushed
1 pound bok choy, torn in bite-size pieces
½ cup oyster mushrooms, halved
if large
½ cup shiitake mushrooms,
halved if large
2 tablespoons oyster sauce

SERVES 4

1 Put the dried black mushrooms in a bowl. Pour the boiling water over them and let soak and soften for about 15 minutes. Drain the mushrooms thoroughly.

2 Heat the wok, then add the oil. When the oil is hot, add the crushed garlic and stir-fry over medium heat until softened but not colored.

3 Add the bok choy and stir-fry for 1 minute. Mix in the mushrooms and stir-fry for 1 minute.

4 Drizzle the oyster sauce over the mixture, toss well and serve immediately.

Stir-fried Vegetables with Cilantro Omelet

INGREDIENTS

1 tablespoon cornstarch
2 tablespoons soy sauce
1 tablespoon sweet chili sauce
½ cup vegetable stock
2 tablespoons peanut oil
1 teaspoon grated fresh ginger
6-8 scallions, sliced
1 cup sugar snap peas
1 yellow bell pepper, seeded and sliced
*1 cup fresh shiitake or
white mushrooms*
*½ cup drained canned water
chestnuts, rinsed*
2 cups bean sprouts
½ small Chinese cabbage, coarsely shredded
OMELET
2 eggs
2 tablespoons water
3 tablespoons chopped fresh cilantro
1 tablespoon peanut oil
salt and freshly ground black pepper

SERVES 3–4

1 Make the omelet. Whisk the eggs, water, cilantro and seasoning in a small bowl. Heat the oil in a wok. Pour in the eggs, then tilt the wok so the mixture spreads to an even layer. Cook over high heat until the edges are slightly crisp.

2 With a wok spatula, flip the omelet over. Cook the other side for 30 seconds, until it is lightly browned. Turn the omelet onto a board and let cool. When cold, roll the omelet up loosely and cut across into thin slices. Set the omelet strands aside. Wipe the wok clean, using paper towels.

3 In a bowl, combine the cornstarch, soy sauce, chili sauce and stock. Set aside.

4 Heat the wok until hot. Add the oil and swirl it around, then add the ginger and scallions and stir-fry for a few seconds to flavor the oil. Add the sugar snap peas, pepper, mushrooms and water chestnuts  and stir-fry for 3 minutes over fairly high heat.

5 Add the beansprouts and the coarsely shredded Chinese cabbage. Stir-fry for 2 minutes.

6 Pour in the cornstarch mixture, stir to mix, then cook, stirring, for about 1 minute, until the glaze thickens and coats the vegetables. Turn the vegetables onto a warmed serving plate and arrange the omelet strands on top. Serve immediately.

48

Crispy "Seaweed" with Slivered Almonds

INGREDIENTS

1 pound collard greens
peanut oil, for deep frying
¼ teaspoon sea salt
1 teaspoon sugar
½ cup slivered almonds, toasted

SERVES 4

1 Remove and discard the thick white stalks from the spring greens. Also discard discolored leaves.

2 Lay several leaves on top of one another, roll up tightly and slice into thread-like strips.

3 Half-fill a deep wok with oil and heat to 350°F. Deep-fry the spring greens in batches for about 1 minute, until they darken and become crisp. Remove each batch from the wok as soon as it is ready and drain on paper towels.

4 Transfer the "seaweed" to a serving dish, sprinkle with the salt and sugar, then mix well. Scatter the toasted almonds over the top and serve.

Deep-fried Root Vegetables with Spiced Salt

INGREDIENTS

1 carrot, cut in long, thin ribbons
2 parsnips, cut in long, thin ribbons
2 beets, cut in thin rounds
1 sweet potato, cut in thin rounds
peanut oil, for deep frying
¼ teaspoon chili powder
1 teaspoon sea salt

SERVES 4–6

51

1 Half-fill a wok with oil and heat to 350°F. Add the vegetable slices in batches and deep-fry for 2–3 minutes, until crisp. Remove and drain well.

2 Place the chili powder and sea salt in a mortar and grind to a coarse powder.

3 Pile up the vegetable crisps on a serving plate and sprinkle the spiced salt on top. Serve at once.

COOK'S TIP
To save time you can also slice the vegetables using a mandolin or food processor with a thin slicing disc attached. Other root vegetables also work well in this recipe.

Yu Hsiang Eggplant in Spicy Sauce

INGREDIENTS

3–4 whole dried red chilies, soaked in water
for 10 minutes
vegetable oil, for deep-frying
1 pound eggplants, cut in short strips
1 garlic clove, finely chopped
1 teaspoon finely chopped fresh ginger
1 teaspoon finely chopped scallion,
white part only
4 ounces lean pork, thinly shredded
1 tablespoon light soy sauce
1 teaspoon light brown sugar
1 tablespoon chili bean sauce
1 tablespoon Chinese rice wine or dry sherry
1 tablespoon rice vinegar
2 teaspoons cornstarch, mixed to a paste with
1 tablespoon water
a few drops sesame oil
1 teaspoon finely chopped scallions, green part
only, to garnish

SERVES 4

1 Drain the soaked red chilies well, cut them into small pieces and discard the seeds.

2 Heat the oil in a wok and deep-fry the eggpant strips for 3–4 minutes, or until limp. Remove and drain on paper towels.

3 Leave I tablespoon of oil in the wok. Add the garlic, ginger, scallion and chilies. Stir well. Add the pork and stir-fry until it is cooked. Add all the seasonings. Bring  to a boil. Add the eggplant and braise for 40 seconds, then thicken with the cornstarch paste. Add the scallions. Sprinkle with the sesame oil. Serve.

Braised Chinese Vegetables

INGREDIENTS

¼ ounce wood ears
8 ounces tofu, cut in 12 small pieces
3-4 tablespoons vegetable oil
¾ cup straw mushrooms, drained
and halved if large
¾ cup sliced bamboo shoots, drained
½ cup sugar snap peas,
trimmed
6 ounces Chinese greens, cut in small pieces
1 teaspoon salt
½ teaspoon light brown sugar
1 tablespoon light soy sauce
a few drops sesame oil (optional)

SERVES 4

1 Put the wood ears in a bowl of cold water to soak for 20–25 minutes, then rinse and discard the hard stalks, if there are any.

2 Add the tofu to a pan of boiling water and leave for 2 minutes until hardened. Drain. Heat the oil in a wok. Stir-fry the tofu until it is golden brown.

3 Using a slotted spoon, remove the tofu from the wok and drain on paper towels. Transfer to a plate and keep hot while you cook the vegetables.

4 Reheat the oil in the wok, add all the vegetables and stir-fry for 1½ minutes. Add the tofu pieces, salt, sugar and soy sauce. Continue to stir-fry for 1 more minute, then cover and braise for 2–3 minutes. Sprinkle with the seasame oil, if using, spoon onto a platter and serve immediately.

Mixed Roasted Vegetables

INGREDIENTS

1 large eggplant cut lengthwise in segments
¾ cup salt, for sprinkling
2 tablespoons olive oil
1 ounce Parmesan cheese, in one piece
2 red bell peppers, seeded and cut lengthwise
in segments
1 yellow bell pepper, seeded and cut lengthwise
in segments
2 plum tomatoes, cut lengthwise in segments
2 tablespoons fresh parsley, chopped
freshly ground black pepper
parsley or cilantro sprigs, to garnish

SERVES 4

1 Place the sliced eggplant in a colander and then sprinkle with salt. Leave for about 30 minutes, to allow the salt to draw out all the bitter juices.

2 Rinse off the salt in cold water, then drain the eggplant well and pat dry with paper towels.

3 Heat the wok. Add 1 teaspoon of the oil. When it is hot, add the Parmesan and stir-fry until golden brown. Remove from the wok and allow it to cool.

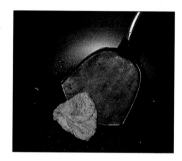

Place the Parmesan on a board and chop into fine pieces, using a cleaver or sharp knife.

4 Heat the wok, then add the rest of the oil. When the oil is hot, stir-fry the eggplant and the peppers for 4–5 minutes. Add the tomatoes and stir-fry for 1

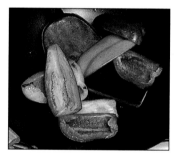

more minute. Toss the vegetables with the Parmesan cheese and the chopped parsley. Add black pepper to taste. Transfer to a platter, garnish with sprigs of parsley or cilantro and serve immediately.

Rice & Noodle Dishes

Crispy Noodles with Mixed Vegetables

INGREDIENTS

peanut oil, for deep frying
1 cup dried vermicelli rice noodles,
broken in 3-inch lengths
1 cup green beans, trimmed and cut
in short lengths
1 inch fresh ginger, cut in shreds
1 fresh red chili, seeded and sliced
1½ cups fresh shiitake or white mushrooms,
thickly sliced
2 large carrots, cut in matchsticks
2 zucchini, cut in matchsticks
a few Chinese cabbage leaves, coarsely shredded
1½ cups bean sprouts
4 scallions, shredded
2 tablespoons light soy sauce
2 tablespoons Chinese rice wine
1 teaspoon sugar
2 tablespoons roughly torn cilantro leaves

SERVES 3–4

1 Half-fill a deep wok with peanut oil. Heat it to 350°F. Deep-fry the noodles, a handful at a time, for 1–2 minutes until puffed and crispy. Drain on paper towels. Carefully pour off all but 2 tablespoons of the oil. Reheat this, then add the beans and stir-fry for 2–3 minutes. Add the ginger shreds, chili, mushrooms, carrots and zucchini and stir-fry for 1–2 minutes.

2 Add the Chinese cabbage, bean sprouts and scallions to the wok. Mix well, then stir-fry the mixture for 1 minute over high heat.

3 Add the soy sauce, rice wine and sugar. Stir-fry for 30 seconds, then lightly toss in all the noodles and the cilantro. Serve the noodles piled on a plate.

Thai Fried Rice

INGREDIENTS

generous 1 cup Thai jasmine rice
6 cups boiling water
1 red bell pepper, seeded
12 ounces skinless, boneless chicken breasts
3 tablespoons vegetable oil
1 onion, chopped
1 garlic clove, crushed
1 tablespoon mild curry paste
½ teaspoon paprika
½ teaspoon ground turmeric
2 tablespoons Thai fish sauce (nam pla)
2 eggs, beaten
salt and freshly ground black pepper
deep fried basil leaves, to garnish

SERVES 4

1 Wash the rice well, drain it and put it in a heavy saucepan. Add the boiling water, return to a boil, and then simmer for about 10 minutes, until just tender. Drain well in a colander, then spread out the grains on a baking sheet and let cool.

2 Cut the red pepper and the chicken breasts into ¾ inch cubes. Heat a wok, then add 2 tablespoons of the oil and swirl it around. Add the onion and red pepper and stir-fry for 1 minute.

3 Add the chicken, garlic, curry paste and spices and stir-fry for 2–3 minutes.

4 Reduce the heat to medium, add the cooled rice, fish sauce and seasoning. Stir-fry for 2–3 minutes, until the rice is very hot.

5 Make a well in the center of the rice and add the rest of the oil. When hot, add the beaten eggs, let cook for 2 minutes, until the eggs are just lightly set, then stir them into the rice mixture, using a spatula or a pair of bamboo chopsticks.

6 Scatter the deep-fried basil leaves on top, and serve immediately, straight from the wok.

Noodles in Soup

INGREDIENTS

12 ounces dried egg noodles
2½ cups chicken stock
2 tablespoons vegetable oil
2 scallions, thinly shredded
*8 ounces chicken breast, pork fillet, or other
cooked meat, thinly shredded*
*1 cup spinach leaves, lettuce hearts, or Chinese
greens, thinly shredded*
*1 cup drained sliced bamboo shoots,
thinly shredded*
*3-4 dried shiitake mushrooms, soaked, squeezed
dry and shredded (stalks discarded)*
1 teaspoon salt
½ teaspoon light brown sugar
1 tablespoon light soy sauce
2 teaspoons Chinese rice wine or dry sherry
a few drops sesame oil
chili sauce, to serve

SERVES 4

1 Cook the noodles in boiling water according to the instructions on the package, drain, then rinse under cold water. Place in a serving bowl. Bring the stock to a boil, pour it over the noodles and keep hot.

2 Heat the oil in a preheated wok, add the scallions and meat, and stir-fry for about 1 minute.

3 Add the greens, bamboo shoots and mushrooms. Stir-fry for 1 minute, then mix in the salt, sugar, soy sauce, rice wine and sesame oil. Pour the vegetable mixture into the serving bowl, on top of the noodles. Serve immediately with the chili sauce.

60

Singapore Noodles

INGREDIENTS

8 ounces dried egg noodles
3 tablespoons peanut oil
1 onion, chopped
1 inch fresh ginger,
finely chopped
1 garlic clove, finely chopped
1 tablespoon Madras curry powder
1/2 teaspoon salt
4 ounces cooked chicken or pork,
finely shredded
4 ounces cooked peeled shrimp
4 ounces Chinese cabbage leaves, shredded
1 cup bean sprouts
4 tablespoons chicken stock
1-2 tablespoons dark soy sauce
1-2 fresh red chilies, seeded and finely
shredded, to garnish
4 scallions, finely shredded, to garnish

SERVES 4

1 Cook the noodles according to the instructions on the package. Rinse under cold water and drain well. Toss in 1 tablespoon of the oil and set aside. Heat a wok, add the remaining oil and stir-fry the onion, ginger and garlic for about 2 minutes.

2 Stir the curry powder and salt into the vegetables and stir-fry for 30 seconds, then add the noodles, meat and shrimp. Stir-fry for 3–4 minutes.

3 Add the Chinese cabbage and bean sprouts and stir-fry for 2 minutes. Drizzle stock and soy sauce on top. Toss, then garnish with the chilies and scallions.

Chinese Jeweled Rice

INGREDIENTS

1⅔ cups long-grain rice
3¾ cups water
3 tablespoons vegetable oil
1 onion, roughly chopped
1 cup peas, thawed if frozen
4 ounces cooked ham, diced
6 ounces drained canned crabmeat
½ cup drained canned water
chestnuts, cut in cubes
4 dried black Chinese mushrooms, soaked,
drained and diced
2 tablespoons oyster sauce
1 teaspoon sugar
whole chives, to garnish

SERVES 4

62

1 Rinse the rice. Bring the water to a boil in a saucepan, add the rice and cover the pan tightly. Cook over low heat for 12 minutes, then refresh under cold water. Heat the wok, then add half the oil. Stir-fry the rice for 3 minutes, then remove and set aside.

2 Add the remaining oil to the wok. When the oil is hot, add the onion and stir-fry briefly, until it has softened but not colored.

3 Add the rest of the ingredients and stir-fry for 2 minutes. Return the rice to the wok and stir-fry for 3 more minutes. Serve, garnished with chives.

Nutty Rice & Mushroom Stir-fry

INGREDIENTS

1⅔ cups long-grain rice
3-3¾ cups water
3 tablespoons sunflower oil
1 small onion, roughly chopped
2 cups Portabello mushrooms, sliced
½ cup hazelnuts, roughly chopped
½ cup pecans, roughly chopped
½ cup almonds, roughly chopped
4 tablespoons chopped fresh parsley
salt and freshly ground black pepper
parsley sprigs, to garnish

SERVES 4–6

4 Add all the nuts and stir-fry for 1 minute. Add the rice to the wok and stir-fry for about 3 minutes. Season. Stir in the parsley. Garnish with parsley sprigs and serve.

1 Rinse the rice. Bring the water to a boil in a saucepan with a tight-fitting lid. Add the rice, cover and cook for 10–12 minutes. When it is cooked, refresh under cold water. Heat the wok, then add half the oil. When the oil is hot, stir-fry the rice for 2–3 minutes. Remove and set aside.

2 Add the remaining oil to the wok and stir-fry the onion for 2 minutes until softened.

3 Mix in the field mushrooms and stir-fry for 2 minutes over high heat.

Index